The Sacred Treasury of the LORD

John Elias Yaakov

authorHOUSE®

AuthorHouse™
1663 Liberty Drive
Bloomington, IN 47403
www.authorhouse.com
Phone: 1 (800) 839-8640

This book represents my own personal testimony and has not been authorized as a works by the Church of Jesus Christ of Latter Day Saints or any other organized church, group or assembly. It is my personal testimony of a personal event, which occurred in my life in July 1997.

Published by AuthorHouse 10/11/2017

ISBN: 978-1-5462-1055-9 (sc)
ISBN: 978-1-5462-1056-6 (e)

Print information available on the last page.

This book is printed on acid-free paper.

Table of Contents

Website designed for:
Windows 7
Internet Explorer 11
Real Player

Melchizzdek

High Priest

The Sacred Treasury of the Lord

Compiled and edited by
John Elias Yaakov

The First Fourteen Books
Compiled in six days

Applying the Key of David
To the New Testament
and the Book of Mormon
"URGENT"

Life – Early Years

I was born on October 9, 1941 at Fort Jackson located in South Carolina, a major training center to this day for the United States Army. My father had shipped out before my birth pursuant to his duties in the South Pacific, in leading-edge electronics and radio communications for the United States Army Signal Core.

The happiest days of my life were my preschool years i.e. (1st picture) growing up in a suburb of Savannah, Georgia?

Both of us, with our vivid imaginations, my friend and I reenacted a scene from a cowboy movie of the day. A smoke screen was created by tying a bundle of tumble weed to a horse to escape the attacking bad guys. We had no horse or tumble weed so using our family dog (as our horse) to pull a long, long rope to which we attached an oily rag which we then set a flame. It was then our dog (Butch) thought the burning rag was chasing him and thus we torched a very large number of straw fields, common to the area. The rope finally broke free from Butch whom we recovered and headed for our tree house hide away realizing by that time with the all the fire trucks, our mothers had an all points search going for our little behinds.

The Story behind the reveal …
The words of the LORD are pure words: as silver tried in a furnace of earth, purified seven times.

Jumping now to 12 years later in 1958 while still in high school a 17- year-old senior class student I joined the Georgia National Guard. I was released from the guard to enter the United States Air Force in 1959.

The Story behind the reveal ...
The words of the LORD are pure words: as silver tried in a furnace of earth, purified seven times.

Life – Military

I served in SAC during the cold war period which included the Cuban Missile Crisis 1959 - 1963

Life - Career

After my tour in the military, I returned to civilian life as a production process operator by day, while attending college classes by night an effort spanning over ten years. During this period, I qualified for and obtained my professional Engineering license from two states. My career has involved me in positions requiring process operations, swing shifts, and meeting manufacturing specifications, testing in a lab environment several days a week. I have held many positions during my career from online operations, event scheduling to shift Supervisor. Planned and supported plant shut downs and startups. With a sound basis in production and operations my career moved into design engineering and process applications design and later into management. Among these management positions was Vice President for a small engineering and construction firm in Atlanta, Georgia. In this position, I supervised directed and developed internal procedural changes to improve efficiency and reduce costs, of human resources, and administrative staff of the company. I have functioned as the Chief Engineer of a company where I setup design and engineering controls to assure the profitability and improvement of controls and schedule for all projects within the house and sought in the immediate future. I have functioned as the Department Chief for Control Systems Engineering for two major firms.

I have also performed the job functions of project manager for both firms. Prior to management positions, I held title and responsibility as lead field and project startup engineer for numerous engineering project startups for clean water plants for city water, paper production, newspaper, gift box, toilet and tissue products, tea bag paper, photo film, and food products. I have worked closely with crafts and trades to develop concepts resulting from R&D to working equipment. From 1965 to 1976, my business career was concentrated in the design engineering, hands on positions, of the profession. I held senior lead positions as my knowledge and skills increased with experience. I had responsibility for instrumentation systems installation, checkout and startup management, and customer support.

In 1977, I started active participation in the initial efforts of technology research as well as the engineering design and development technology which continues today, slowly, on a proprietary concept from prototype model, of a proofed system, including scheme implementation plans for key control strategies resulting in a reliable final manufactured product. I have obtained three United States patents in pursuit of this technology.

All the projects that I designed, installed and supervised met both cost and predefined implementation goals. Throughout my business career I have had profit and loss responsibility, as well as operations and direct sales experience. I [semi-retired] in 2002. I share this with you to show my primary day to day life has been in science involving physics and engineering skills.

The Story behind the reveal …
The words of the LORD are pure words: as silver tried in a furnace of earth, purified seven times.

Life - Patents

The spiritual events of July 1997 came totally unexpected. As a Registered Professional Engineer, I have always had to be responsible for my doings for the safety of my fellow man. The rebuke of this event by the sitting church authority was also unexpected and personally very painful. I have prayed and continued my efforts humbly in the hope that by hearing you will be in awe and agree with me that no man could accomplish this without divine intervention.

Life – Faith

As to my faith I was born the third son of my mother who frequented the Methodist Church and my father the Lutheran Church. After his return from World War II in the South Pacific, he seldom attended services and eventually over time completely abstained. I attended services with my mother until my mid-teens. I was not satisfied and felt I needed more in my faith and became Roman Catholic where I was satisfied for twenty-four years.

But with the maturity of life brings with it realities and trials. I found myself denied from the practice of my faith by tenet and the catechism of the church. Approximately nine years later I was baptized and married in the Temple of The Church of Jesus Christ of Latter Day Saints. My wife and young adult children enjoyed our participation in the LDS church tenets and social activities and interface with the congregation members. I am presently a High Priest in The Church of Jesus Christ of Latter Day Saints (LDS).

A few lines extracted from Patriarchal Blessing Number 229:

Brother-_____, be-strong-and-of-good courage, because <u>much is expected of you.</u>

You will be called upon to serve in various positions of responsibility and trust in the Church as you continue to keep the commandments of our Father in Heaven. Be kind, be gentle, be patient, and all good things will come to you.

Again, I admonish you to remain close to our Heavenly Father. He has much work for you to do, <u>and only you can do it.</u>

Religious Event

My faith has increased but my progress slowed due to a religious event which I reported through the proper channel protocols of the church to the authorities sitting in the highest offices of the faith.

After their review which never included speaking to me personally, beyond the local leadership, I came to be advised that the authorities were indifferent to my claims and I was not to mention them to the church congregation in testimony or discussion on church properties. This action placing me and my soul in a paradox; "Do I believe GOD or do I believe man". A status I hold today and the authorities sequester of my testimony before the church has prevailed over my testimony for 21 years this coming July 2018. After sixteen years this had pasted in July 2013 and current events in our country and the world, and after much prayer I am writing this book of the works I believe God blessed me in July 1997 to accomplish. A reveal of his works to aide all that follow Jesus Christ in seeking redemption and salvation for the world through his great and marvelous works which he has done by his on hand. I am the steward for these reveals which occurred in July 1997 and I am pursuing the ends of these efforts to make them known to the world. It was twenty years ago this past July 2017 ...

This whole matter began in my conscious mind when on July 17, 1997 with my faith not being on my mind; an acquaintance (with a first name of David) in and automobile repair shop approached me with a question about quantum physics. Knowing that I was a Professional Engineer, he reasoned that I might be able to answer a few basic questions he had on the subject. After some technical discussions and having answered his questions to the best of my ability our discussion took a new path which seemed to me a bit odd. He told me of some happenings and presented me with a paper on which was written a verse. It struck me at the time that the writing was not recognizable as scripture but none the less of apparent profound origin. He asked me what I thought of the writings and asked me to see if they were scripture or even close. I checked the verse against scripture on the computer and could not find anything even promising. I pondered this for several days and returned to speak to him again on July 21, 1997 and he again presented me with writing. I asked him where they came from and he said I jot them down as they come into my head. I asked him why he was bringing these writings to me. He said, he did not know why, but he knew he was supposed to tell these things to me. He was now becoming somewhat agitated. I asked him was there anything else that he was supposed to tell me that he had not written down. He said, "Only, that all would be revealed in the circle of the twenty-one

The Story behind the reveal ...
The words of the LORD are pure words: as silver tried in a furnace of earth, purified seven times.

stones. Then he asks me to leave him alone about it. He had no idea what it meant, but whatever. Now this man is not of any church active. I have touched on the subject and he rebukes it. He does not wish to discuss it, as it is not for him. I returned to my house wherein my office is and pondered what I had heard and seen. After much consideration of other things, I was about to set it aside when it struck me as a flash that tablets have been in stone for record keeping. Modern Books have TABS; Scriptures have tabs, which mark the Books therein. I opened my New Testament Scriptures and was amazed to find seven tabs each containing three books for a total of twenty-one. I opened my Church of Jesus Christ of Latter Day Saints, Book of Mormon Scriptures and was amazed to find seven tabs each containing three books if you count the D&C 1-49 is a Tab, 50-99 is a Tab, and 100 - 138 is a Tab. Further, I was even more amazed. I will remember always the day of July 21, 1997 as a most unusual day when I began to get flashes that were spiritual in nature and these continued up until the night of my actual experience. I had attended our Stake Social earlier in the evening and retired about Midnight July 26, 1997. I was set upon, about 3:00 A.M., half-awake and half-asleep, I became aware of dark forces whirling it seemed, about my head, but most assuredly in my mind and I was so frightened. So much so, that I wanted to call on the LORD immediately, for I knew this was an evil presence I was feeling. I have known the LORD'S PRAYER ever since I was a little boy, so in me frighten state I wanted to pray this prayer as part of my plea for help. My mind was in such disarray that I could not remember the words, only the desire to say them at that very moment. Now terrified,

The Story behind the reveal ...
The words of the LORD are pure words: as silver tried in a furnace of earth, purified seven times.

and most assuredly wide-awake, I made my way as quietly as I could down the dark hall of our home. I wanted to take this problem from my bedroom to my home office. I went to my computer where I have a complete set Of LDS Scriptures and quickly sought to look up prayers. As my body trembled and shook I still could not find the LORD'S PRAYER, but I found a list of Names and Prayers to Jesus Christ. The first was ADVOCATE, which I selected. The Prayers of our Lord in Gethsemane appeared on my screen and I received a warmth and loss of the evil presence, being replaced by a feeling of love. My computer begins to behave most strangely when the Prayers of our Lord in Gethsemane appeared on my CRT screen. I was then asked on screen if I would drink from the bitter cup for the LORD? I was asked twice, to which a keyboard yes or no was required.

I answered both times with yes and He, revealing himself as Jesus Christ conversed with me in my mind as my body trembled and shook and after a time my computer screen revealed a sequence of how to discern the compiled scriptures. He said in this sequence he would speak to us anew. I was to compile the New Testament and the Book of Mormon and take them to my Bishop, which I did in six days. I had no visual contact with anyone or thing, only a strong presence of love for me and all true believers in Jesus Christ's gospel and true church. I know what happened to me and I only wish us to receive all the blessings our father in heaven has prepared for us. In professing our faith, I feel we must be careful not to overlook major blessings as mere chance or coincidence. I know that all the scriptures revealed to us and those given in the D&C to the Prophet Joseph Smith, Jr. were from the Lord.

The Story behind the reveal …
The words of the LORD are pure words: as silver tried in a furnace of earth, purified seven times.

These compiled versus yield a new works of the LORD written of his own finger for the salvation of all his children. When this event occurred in our home July 1997 the first two sections (The Bible New Testament (KJV) & The Church of Jesus Christ of Latter Day Saints Church Book of Mormon) were to be done immediately and the third (Old Testament) could be done at my own pace. I stopped work on everything and began the work, awakened each morning at three o'clock AM and rolled out of bed in a position of prayer. I say again that I delivered the first two sections to my Bishop in six days. Remember, I wrote not one word in any of the books. They were all compiled under the influence of the Holy Spirit of Promise over a period of six days. My family and a few close friends have witnessed this event and we all stand in awe of the Lord.

Neither the Bishop nor the Stake President has allowed me to bear my testimony concerning this matter. I believe there are only two churches on the face of the earth and they are the church of the Devil and the church of Jesus Christ, which means that all who accept Jesus Christ as their Lord and Savior are members of the body of Christ as Denominations are only degrees or levels of enlightenment. However, I continue steadfast in The Church of Jesus Christ of Latter Day Saints Church as I believe I am here but by the will and Grace of God to affect the fulfillment of prophecy.

After many sessions and meetings with my stake president everything was returned to me declaring I had no authority to receive this material for the church. I have held my place and continued my duties within the church.

The Story behind the reveal …
The words of the LORD are pure words: as silver tried in a furnace of earth, purified seven times.

Asking the Lord each night to guide me and in his due time to show me his will as it is to be done. The rest of the works are to remain sealed on my shelf until the Lord's own due time.

wThe organized church has reacted as if I am in error, a foolish overzealous convert to the Lords church, yet, I know what I know and Heavenly Father must have a plan that will reveal itself in his own due time.

Do I believe God or do I believe man? A paradox with eternal implications requires patience, prayer, patience and then more prayer. Thus, here we stand today, seven months away from the 21st anniversary of this event, and again I believe by providence, exercising our free agency, praying each day, not my will, but his will be done. I was revisited by the Spirit October 1st and 2nd 2011 with the message that time have run out for those responsible for keeping it from you. I wrote NOT ONE WORD ... so, it was NOT for me alone which I have said ... peace be with you. GLORY to the FATHER in his HOLY name even JESUS CHRIST AMEN!

Now with this printed, I again wait for the word on how to proceed with the remainder of my life. For my peace of mind and in faith, I continue to place this matter in the hands of the Lord. I continue to scratch out a living while proceeding ever so slowly with my engineering research now in its forty-fifth year and have come to learn that the pace of progress in this endeavor is also in the hands of the Lord.

It moves forward much like a chain that is being pulled up a hill where by pushing it, is to no avail. Nothing I can do

The Story behind the reveal ...
The words of the LORD are pure words: as silver tried in a furnace of earth, purified seven times.

seems to speed things up yet I must hold tight to the chain lest I lose the pace of positive progress. As to my research engineering, we wait now for a certain classified material formula to cast the last part of the machine core. This may call for a special group for one year.

The basics of the 1997 event, if you consider Ephraim [Book 14] verse 748 which [748 is also the Gematria for the fullness of Yaakov] which assigns me stewardship for this work and is followed by verse 749 which names this set of books as "The Sacred Treasury of the Lord" The first fourteen books.

They were compiled using the sequence declared in Rueben [Book 01] as the Key of David (KoD) from the Bible (King James Version) The New Testament and the Book of Mormon from The Church of Jesus Christ of Latter Day Saints.

The Story behind the reveal ...
The words of the LORD are pure words: as silver tried in a furnace of earth, purified seven times.

Mothers House

My Mother's maiden name is Kobbe. My DNA testing shows Solomon as second cousins to this German surname of Kobbe.

KOBBE was derived amazingly from Hebrew given name Yaakov, via the Latin Jacobus. In the Bible, this is the name of the younger twin brother of Esau who took advantage of the lack of hunger and impetuousness to persuade him to part with his birthright 'for a mess of potage'. The name is traditionally interpreted as coming from Hebrew AKEV (heel) and Jacob is said to have been born holding on to Esau's heel. The name has travelled widely and the principal forms of the given name in major European languages are Jacob, Jacques, Koop, Hupka, Kubica and Iacopo, to name but a few. Throughout Eastern Europe Jewish forms of the name were extremely common, ranging from Yaakov to Jankl. The first hereditary surnames on German soil are found in the second half of the 12th century, slightly later than in England and France. However, it was not until the 16th century that they became stabilized. The practice of adopting hereditary surnames began in the southern areas of Germany, and gradually spread northwards during the Middle Ages.

A notable member of the name was John Jacob (years 1812 to 1858) a British military officer in India, where he had the name 'ag Kanghur' changed to Jacobbas in 1851 in his honor. Because of the close relationship between the English and German languages, some Germans can transform their names to the English form just by dropping a single letter. Many Germans have re-spelt their names in America. After the start of the first World War, Germans in great numbers Anglicized their names to remove all doubt as to their patriotism.

Afterwards some changed back, and then during World War II the problem became acute once more, and the changing started all over again, although not with as much intensity. Many immigrants from Germany settled in Pennsylvania. In the Middle Ages heraldry came into use as a practical matter. It originated in the devices used to distinguish the armored warriors in tournament and war, and was also placed on seals as marks of identity. As far as records show, true heraldry began in the middle of the 12ᵗʰ century, and appeared almost simultaneously in several countries of Western Europe.

An unorthodox branch of Judaism which maintains that Jesus is the Jewish Messiah whose coming was foretold by Old Testament prophets.

The emblem of the Melchizedek adherent of Messianic Judaism, adherent of an Priesthood of the Church of Latter-Day Saints, who view it as a continuation of the priesthood of biblical patriarchs. The emblem is patterned after a similar glyph found in a medieval depiction of Melchizedek but is of relatively recent usage by The Church of Jesus Christ of Latter Day Saints (LDS). The star in this context would most likely have been a symbol of renewal and rebirth through baptism. The eight-pointed silver star on a gold infinity symbol running up the center of the shield claiming immeasurableness, eternity boundlessness; infinite space or size; infinite amount.

This is a perfect priesthood continuing forever unlike the old which changed, this is administered by the eternal Son of God to all who are in the house of God (Hebrews 9:15-10:21). the Melchizedek Priesthood forever. The same Melchizedak Priesthood of our Lord and savior Jesus Christ, the King of Kings.

Melchizedek

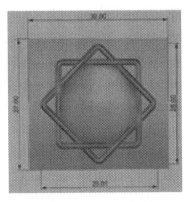

[Zion take notice!)

The Story behind the reveal …
The words of the LORD are pure words: as silver tried in a furnace of earth, purified seven times.

Fleur-de-lis Blood line of the Blessed Trinity. The fleur-de-lis or fleur-de-lis in French literally means lily flower? (fleur means flower, and lis means lily or iris). However, let me state that when you see this symbol emblazoned today on various flags or engraved on royal crowns, the fleur-de-lis does not represent the lily flower, but the Trinity of the Brotherhood. For it is an emblem of a blood line of divine majesty and the symbol of a royal Brotherhood that had originated long before the foundation of Rome, or the founding royal houses of France.

MY MOTHERS HOUSE

Messianic Jew

My DNA shows I am second cousin to Solomon

The Story behind the reveal …
The words of the LORD are pure words: as silver tried in a furnace of
earth, purified seven times.

The First Seven Books:
"Urgent" 01 - 07

Book of Rueben[01]

Bookof Simeon[02]

Book of Levi [03]

Book of Judah [04]

Book of Dan [05]

Book of Naphtali [06]

Book of Gad [07]

The first seven books were compiled from the New Testament applying the Key of David as the sequence is named when you listen to the audio of the Book of Rueben-01 on my website. http://www.thehosscampus.com Home-of-the-Second-Forerunner.

Whom they refused

This Moses whom they refused, saying, who made thee a ruler and a judge? the same did God send [to be] a ruler and a deliverer by the hand of the angel which appeared to him in the bush. But refuse profane and old wives' fables, and exercise thyself [rather] unto godly-ness. By faith Moses, when he was come to years, refused to be called the son of Pharaoh's daughter; He began to repent of the evil which he had done; he began to remember the words which had been spoken by the mouth of all the prophets, and he saw them that they were fulfilled thus far, every whit; and his soul mourned and refused to be comforted. For not many days hence and the earth shall tremble and reel to–and-fro as a drunken man; and the sun shall hide his face, and shall refuse to give light; and the moon shall be bathed in blood; and the stars shall become exceedingly angry, and shall cast themselves down as a fig that fall from off a fig-tree. They kept not the covenant of God, and refused to walk in his law; Because I have called, and ye refused; I have stretched out my hand, and no man regarded; He [is in] the way of life that keep instruction: but he that refuse reproof errs. The robbery of the wicked shall destroy them; because they refuse to do judgment. The things [that] my soul refused to touch [are] as my sorrowful meat. Thou hast made us [as] the off scouring and refuse amid the people. And refused to obey, neither were mindful of thy wonders that thou didst among them; but hardened their necks, and in their rebellion appointed a captain to return to their bondage: but thou [art] a God ready to pardon, gracious and merciful, slow to anger, and of great kindness, and forsook them not. But the LORD said unto Samuel, look not on his countenance, or on the height of his stature; because I have refused him: for [the LORD see's not as man see's; for man looks on the outward appearance, but the LORD looks on the heart. And a certain man of the sons of the prophets said unto his neighbor in the word of the LORD, smite me, I pray thee. And the man refused to smite him. Therefore, the showers have been withheld, and there hath been no latter rain; and thou had a whore's forehead, thou refused to be ashamed. LORD, [are] not thine eyes upon the truth? thou hast stricken them, but they have not grieved; thou hast consumed them, [but] they have refused to receive correction: they have made their faces harder than a rock; they have refused to return. They are turned back to the iniquities of their forefathers, which refused to hear my words; and they went after other gods to serve them: the house of Israel and the house of Judah have broken my covenant which I made with their fathers. This evil people, which refuse to hear my words, which walk in the imagination of their heart, and walk after other gods, to serve them, and to worship them, shall even be as this girdle, which is good for nothing. And it shall be, if they refuse to take the cup at thine hand to drink, then shalt thou say unto them, thus saith the LORD of hosts; Ye shall certainly drink. But if thou refuse to go forth, this [is] the word that the LORD hath shewed me: And all his sons and all his daughters rose to comfort him; but he

The Story behind the reveal …
The words of the LORD are pure words: as silver tried in a furnace of earth, purified seven times.

refused to be comforted; and he said, For I will go down into the grave unto my son mourning. Thus, his father wept for him. And the LORD said unto [this] Moses, Pharaoh's [sitting Prophet] heart [is] hardened, he refuses to let the people go. And [this] Moses and [his] Aaron came in unto Pharaoh, and said unto him, thus saith the LORD God of the Hebrews, how long wilt thou refuse to humble thyself before me? **Let my people go, that they may serve me.**

The shields represent the audio books waiting for you to listen to on my website.

The Story behind the reveal …
The words of the LORD are pure words: as silver tried in a furnace of earth, purified seven times.

The Second Seven Books: "Urgent" 08 - 14

Book-of-Asher-08]

Book of Issachar [09]

Book of Zebulon [10]

Book of Benjamin [11]

Book of Joseph [12]

The Story behind the reveal ...
The words of the LORD are pure words: as silver tried in a furnace of
earth, purified seven times.

Book of Manasseh [13]

Book of Ephraim [14]

The second seven books were compiled from the Book of Mormon applying the Key of David [KoD] as the sequence is named when you listen to the audio of the Book of Rueben-01 on my website.

The Key Of David

01	02	03	04	05	06	07	08	09	10	11	12	13	14	15	16	17	18	19	20	21
		3	>	+	>	4			3	>	+	>	4			3	>	+	>	4
						v							v							v
						v							v							v
						7							7							7

The scriptures which are perfect pair sets were sealed in the Bible verses and are now liberated for your eyes to see and your ears to hear http://www.thehosscampus.com

Home-Second-Forerunner.

Little scripture is written here in this book as it would count against me as an author and would delete my ownership of the content. This book is intended to take you to the website to listen. I tried twice to have the book published but was impossible to get the publisher to understand it was the pairing and sequence of the versus that made the resulting read. If they could find the verse in the bible it was not mine. Thankfully the copyright office saw the sequence and issued. I have printed myself, in my own office seven (7) stitched leather-bound text numbered 1-of-7 thru 7-of-7. The perfect paired verse sets read fluidly when compiled by the Key of David sequence [KoD]. I gave Book 1of7 to the Stake President for the for the LDS Church and I kept book 7-of-7 for myself. The reading of the text has clear message delivery and rhythm to the flow of the spoken word. It compiled successfully the sequence selected versus of the New Testament, the Book of Mormon and the Old Testament. In physics, the KoD sequence is called a synchronicity. The pair sets all have Sum of 7.

I made seven copies of the text bound in leather. picture is book 7 of 7

For this is he that was spoken of by the prophet Esaias, saying, the voice of one crying in the wilderness, prepare ye the way of the Lord, make his paths straight. And there was delivered unto him the book of the prophet Esaias. And when he had opened the book, he found the place where it was written and he began to say unto them, this day is this scripture fulfilled in your ears. And he said, Verily I say unto you, no prophet is accepted in his own country. For I say unto you, among those that are born of women there is not a greater prophet than John the Baptist: but he that is least in the kingdom of God is greater than he. Then those men, when they had seen the miracle that Jesus did, said, this is of a truth that prophet that should come into the world. That the saying of Esaias the prophet might be fulfilled, which he spoke, Lord, who hath believed our report? and to whom hath the arm of the Lord been revealed? And he spoke also concerning a prophet who should come before the Messiah, to prepare the way of the Lord—

Wherefore I spoke unto them, saying: Hear ye the words of the prophet, ye who are a remnant of the house of Israel, a branch who have been broken off; hear ye the words of the prophet, which were written unto all the house of Israel, and liken them unto yourselves, that ye may have hope as well as your brethren from whom ye have been broken off; for after this manner has the prophet written. And now, I declare unto you that this prophet of whom Moses spoke was the Holy One of Israel; wherefore, he shall execute judgment in righteousness. And the people began to look with great earnestness for the sign which had been given by the prophet Samuel, the Lamanite, yea, for the time that there should be darkness for the space of three days over the face of the land. And then the words of the prophet Isaiah shall be fulfilled, which say: this day is this scripture fulfilled in your ears. And he said, Verily I say unto you, no prophet is accepted in his own country. For I say unto you, among those that are born of women there is not a greater prophet than John the Baptist: but he that is least in the kingdom of God is greater than he. Then those men, when they had seen the miracle that Jesus did, said, this is of a truth; that prophet that should come into the world. And again, in connection with this quotation I will give you a quotation from one of the prophets, who had his eye fixed on the restoration of the priesthood, the glories to be revealed in the last days, and in an especial manner this most glorious of all subjects belonging to the everlasting gospel, namely, the baptism for the dead; for Malachi says, last chapter, verses 5th and 6th: Behold, I will send you Elijah the prophet before the coming of the great and dreadful day of the Lord: And he shall turn the heart of the fathers to the children, and the heart of the children to their fathers, lest I come and smite the earth with a curse. And upon them that hearken not to the voice of the Lord shall be fulfilled that which was written by the prophet Moses, that they should be cut off from among the people.

Joseph Smith, the Prophet and Seer of the Lord, has done more, save Jesus only, for the salvation of men in this world, than any other man that ever lived in it. In the short space of twenty years, he has brought forth the Book of Mormon, which he translated by the gift and power of God, and has been the means of publishing it on two continents; has sent the fulness of the everlasting gospel, which it contained, to the four quarters of the earth; has brought forth the revelations and commandments which compose this book of Doctrine and Covenants, and many other wise documents and instructions for the benefit of the children of men; gathered many thousands of the Latter-day Saints, founded a great city, and left a fame and name that cannot be slain. He lived great, and he died great in the eyes of God and his people; and like most of the Lord's anointed in ancient time, has sealed his mission and his works with his own blood; and so, has his brother Hyrum. In life they were not divided,

The Story behind the reveal ...
The words of the LORD are pure words: as silver tried in a furnace of
earth, purified seven times.

and in death they were not separated!

The work of Zion is not completed and the efforts of Joseph Smith Jr, to establish the temple in Jackson county Missouri goes unfinished.

A grievous sin unto the Lord, who has claimed this house where he will manifest himself there and the Golden Temple that will come down out of heaven into Israel. His Kingdom on Earth will be administered from these two temples.

The Story behind the reveal …
The words of the LORD are pure words: as silver tried in a furnace of earth, purified seven times.

The Third Seven Books: "My Pace" 15 – 21

The following Books:

15 – 21

Compiled by the Key of David

Can be found as the gold audio books on the left side of the website

http://www.thehosscampus.com

Home-Second-Forerunner

This section was done at my own pace and was not a part of the "urgent message" which was the first fourteen (14) books which I compiled in six (6) days and delivered to the Bishop of the then third ward for Roanoke VA. July 1997.

I did these books [15-21] for the benefit of the Jewish Faith to show the resulting words compiled using the Key of David. A sequence of numbers when applied form a combination that unlocks sealed sections of scripture that have been there from the beginning of the word as written.

Vision/Day Dream

During the period that I compiled the Old Testament from the various Jewish Text I had a Vision/Day Dream as I was very tired and may have dozed off a few minutes while compiling these Books 15-21 [Gold Audio Books] on the left side of the website page http://www.thehosscampus.com
Home-Second-Forerunner.

I saw a man sitting in a heavy gold chair wearing priestly garments of pure white stand-up and declared that he was stepping down as God had instructed, for his constant prayers for man were needed in seeking redemption for this wicked world and seventeen years later it happened. Having been a Roman Catholic for24 years I recognized the man as the Roman Catholic Pope.

Key of David

3rd verse

+

4th verse

Pair set = 7

3,7,10,14,17,21

01	02	03	04	05	06	07	08	09	10	11	12	13	14	15	16	17	18	19	20	21
		3	>	+	>	4			3	>	+	>	4			3	>	+	>	4
						v							v							v
						v							v							v
						7							7							7

Received form Jesus Christ the key or
Combination to open the doors to the Kingdom
of God here on earth for a thousand years.

The 7ᵗʰ Day

Even before they were born, they, with many others, received
their first lessons in the world of spirits and were prepared
to come forth in the due time of the Lord to labor in his
vineyard for the salvation of the souls of men. And after they
have paid the penalty of their transgressions, and are washed
clean, shall receive a reward according to their works, for
they are heirs of salvation.

The Story behind the reveal …
The words of the LORD are pure words: as silver tried in a furnace of
earth, purified seven times.

Foot Notes

{fn-01-KoD} Old Testament – Hebrew [Text KoD]

{fn-02-KoD} KJV - New Testament [Text KoD]

{fn-03-KoD} Book of Mormon [Text KoD]

{fn-04 page2} [The Fullness of Yaakov and His Sons - Gematria 748©By Jewish Path Blog on January 16, 2009 4:51 PM- Dr. Akiva Gamliel http://www.jewishpath.org/ jewishpath_blog/2009/01/the-fullness-of-yaakov-and-his-sons-gematria-748.html]

{fn-05 page 2} [NUMBERBITE

Daily number thingies that are easy to digest - Professor Ian Mallett

http://www.fivedoves.com/numberbite/NUMBERBITE

{fn-06 page 2} [Hebrew Gematria: Values of 758: fifth, a fifth part. a destroyer, an ambush (said of troops); Destruction. Copper or Bronze; Worthlessness (figurative meaning relative to gold); a copper thing or article; money; a chain or fetter. Copyright © by Bill Heidrick]

{fn-07}

Audio Books on Website: http://www.thehosscampus.com
Home-of-Second-Forerunner

{fn-08} The House of Names from whom we purchased the background of the name Kobbe.

{fn-9} My Ancestry DNA Testing shows

51.0% German [Messianic Jew]

39.0% Sweden

6.0% Great Britain

2.0% West Asia

2.0% Caucasus Mountains

Sur Names Kobbe – Solomon 2nd Cousins

About the Author

I was born on October 9, 1941 at Fort Jackson located in South Carolina, a major training center to this day for the United States Army. My father had shipped out before my birth pursuant to his duties in the South Pacific, in leading-edge electronics and radio communications for the United States Army Signal Core.

The happiest days of my life were my preschool years i.e. (1st picture) growing up in a suburbs of Savannah, Georgia? Both with our vivid imaginations my friend and I reenacted a scene from a cowboy movie of the day where a smoke screen was created to escape the attacking bad guys using our family dog (our horse) to pull a long, long rope which attached to an oily rag which we then set a flame. It was then our dog (Butch) thought the burning rag was chasing him and thus we torched a very large number of straw fields, common to the area. The rope finally broke free from Butch whom we recovered and headed for our tree house hide away realizing by that time with the all the fire trucks, our mothers had an all points search going for our little behinds.

Jumping now to 17 years later in 1958 while still in high school as a senior class student I joined the Georgia

National Guard. I was released from the guard to enter the United States Air Force in 1959. I served in SAC during the cold war period which included the Cuban Missile Crisis 1959 -1963.

Printed in the United States
By Bookmasters